Goss &
Crested China

A Collector's Guide

GOSS &
Crested China

A Collector's Guide

Lynda Pine

MILLER'S GOSS & CRESTED CHINA: A COLLECTOR'S GUIDE
by Lynda Pine

First published in Great Britain in 2001 by Miller's, a division of
Mitchell Beazley, imprints of Octopus Publishing Group Ltd,
2–4 Heron Quays, London E14 4JP

Miller's is a registered trademark of Octopus Publishing Group Ltd

Commissioning Editor **Anna Sanderson**
Deputy Art Director **Vivienne Brar**
Senior Art Editor **Rhonda Fisher**
Project Editor **Emily Anderson**
Designer **Louise Griffiths**
Editor **Joan Porter**
Proofreader **Laura Hicks**
Indexer **Sue Farr**
Picture Research **Nick Wheldon**
Production **Catherine Lay**
Illustrator **Amanda Patton**
Jacket photography by **Steve Tanner**

ISBN 1 84000 354 5
A CIP catalogue record for this book is available from the British Library
Set in Bembo, Frutiger and Shannon
Produced by Toppan Printing Co., (HK) Ltd.
Printed and bound in China

Jacket illustrations, front cover, clockwise from top left: Carlton "John
Citizen", c.1902–31, £125–135/$200–215; W.H. Goss "Great Pyramid" near
Cairo, c.1890–1929, £90–100/$145–160; W.H. Goss three-handled loving
cup, c.1890–1929, £35–40/$55–65; Arcadian lucky black cats on sledge,
c.1924–39, £200–215/$320–345; **back cover:** Wembley lion on ashtray
base, c.1924–25, £55–65/$90–105; **half-title page:** "Evangeline Goss"
sleeping on a casket, c.1861–2, £300–400/$480–640; **contents page:**
Carlton puppy on a hand mirror, c.1902–30, £85–95/$135–150

contents

Introduction & what to collect

In the early 1880s Adolphus Goss, of the Goss Pottery, spotted a potential market and began to supply one retail outlet in each British seaside town with Goss porcelain miniatures bearing the town's own coat of arms. No one could have predicted the explosion of what then became the biggest collecting craze of the century. Although the popularity of the seaside was well established by the 1850s, the Industrial Revolution and a rapid expansion of the railway system gave workers the freedom to enjoy the pleasures of a day trip to the coast. As the railway infrastructure grew, exclusive agencies selling souvenir Goss sprang up in cities, towns and villages all over Britain.

The souvenir trade became a lifeline to the potting industry of north Staffordshire, and most of the potteries joined in the crested trade, increasing the range from china whelk shells and lighthouses to a variety of interesting and novelty shapes. Unlike the Goss Pottery, they supplied as many outlets as possible, including station stalls, lending libraries, tea rooms and stationers. One rule was maintained

"Bass basket" by W.H. Goss, c.1890–1929, ht 6.5cm/2½in, **£15–18/$25–28**

by all – the local crests could only be bought in the relevant places. So if a crest of Land's End was required, the collector had to go to Land's End in order to buy it. When the potting industry declined into a big depression in the late 19thC, this craze for souvenirs revitalized many firms, which switched production to ornamental miniatures.

Germany and Austria had already captured the market for china dolls, and they too quickly capitalized on the growing souvenir business. Soon there were almost as many foreign-made British souvenirs as there were British ones.

When deciding what to collect, the beginner is faced with a vast range of shapes made over a 50-year period, by over 150 British manufacturers using more than 350 different factory marks, as well as German and Austrian souvenir ware. It is always best to buy what pleases you most. You may prefer to keep to one crest, such as your home town, or you could aim for a particular theme, or the products of a particular pottery – Goss is an easy choice as almost all its pieces are factory-marked.

The "bass basket", left, is a splendid example of Goss quality, delicacy and careful painting of the coat-of-arms. Almost half of all crested china is small vases, jugs, pots and ewers, and these are easily found. Small Goss pieces can be bought for £5/$8, with the crested china examples costing as little as £3/$5. Anything sub-standard will be less than half the price of a perfect piece.

Many antiques shops stock crested china, and antiques fairs, collectors' fairs and car-boot sales all over the country can offer rich pickings, while auction houses, the internet and specialist dealers have a wide selection and are usually reliable over the value and condition of pieces. When buying mail order, take care to ensure that you can return the goods for a full refund if you are not happy with the quality.

of value it does not seem to matter whether the gilding is rubbed or not. Only pay the full price for a perfect piece – damaged pieces can be restored but will never be worth as much. Firing flaws are common, so only very bad manufacturing flaws can reduce the value of an item. Avoid heavy, poorly-made crude crested china – mainly tableware and large ornamental – and do not confuse this with the real thing, the high quality, translucent and delicate ware. When you find a bargain it is a wonderfully satisfying feeling, and you can use your new skills and knowledge to build up a valued collection.

Collecting tip: do not tell all the dealers you come across what pieces you are looking for, as you could find they will raise the price at auction.

Arcadian unglazed busts: HRH Prince of Wales, c.1925–33, ht 13.5cm/5¼in, **£75–85/$120–135**; Queen Mary, c.1911–33, ht 13.5cm/5¼in, **£45–55/$70–90**

About one-third of all crested ware is unmarked, and as your knowledge increases you will be able to identify the manufacturer of any given shape at a glance. Turn a piece of Goss china upside-down and look at the marks on the base. Goss was nearly always factory-marked with its usual black Gosshawk, sometimes on the back. The very early first-period pieces had "W H Goss" impressed on them while the clay was damp.

Always check condition, preferably under a lamp to make sure there are no hairline cracks or chips. Check also for faded crests and, in the case of Goss, rubbed gilding. Other manufacturers' pieces had poor-quality gilding anyway so in terms

Carlton "Radio operator", c.1925, ht 8.5cm/3½in, **£140–160/$225–255**

Prices & dimensions

Prices for antiques vary, depending on the condition of the item, geographical location and market trends, so the price ranges given throughout this book are guides to value only.

The sterling/dollar conversion has been made at a rate of £1 = $1.60 (adjust as necessary to accord with current exchange rates). The abbreviations ht, diam. and l. are used for dimensions.

The Goss Pottery

William Henry Goss acquired his manufacturing skills under the tutelage of his friend Alderman Copeland, for whom he rose to be chief designer at the Copeland Works in Stoke-on-Trent. Goss left in 1852, at the age of 21, to start up on his own in direct competition with Copeland, using the same retail outlets and producing a similar range of parian (see p.60) figures – mostly busts of noteworthy gentlemen, elegant vases and table centrepieces.

William's son, Adolphus, had the idea of making small artefacts, copied from ancient models in museums and decorated with highly coloured enamels, to sell as souvenirs. From its new premises in Sturgess Street, Stoke, the Goss family was inundated with demands from the ever-growing number of souvenir agencies (more than 1,000 in Britain alone), and Adolphus, with his son Dick, also began taking on agencies worldwide.

Parian ware had been invented around 1870–71 by both Minton and Copeland; the ingredients that Goss used were Norwegian and Swedish felspar, white ground glass, flints and kaolin (china clay). Models and shapes were made from moulds by pouring in the liquid clay and then tipping it out to leave a thin lining in the mould. Each piece was made in at least two parts, which were joined together with slip (see p.60). They were then fired, glazed, decorated and then fired again. These simple elegant porcelain shapes, such as the urn and crinkle-top globe vase shown below, were decorated on top of the glaze with enamels. Adolphus designed these early shapes during the 1880s, and they were painted by hand with seaweeds, moths and butterflies, grasses, ancient armour and Oxford and Cambridge colleges – the forerunners of the seaside town crests which began the collecting craze. This Golden Jubilee 1887 commemorative globe vase bears Victoria's initial and is finished with a ribbon inscribed "Jubilee Of Our Beloved Queen".

Goss crested artefacts are usually named on the base, but sometimes on the side or back. All have precise origins, and some of these are incorporated in the descriptions printed on them; for example, the "water bottle" on the opposite page is inscribed on the back "Model of Army Water Bottle used at the Battle of Waterloo". The original version of

Left to right: urn, c.1870–85, ht 9.5cm/3¾in, **£15–20/$25–30**;. globe vase, c.1887, ht 10.5cm/4¼in, **£70–80/$110–130**

Waterloo soldier's "water bottle", c.1890–1929, ht 8.5cm/3⅜in, **£18–20/$28–30**; Nottingham urn, c.1890–1929, ht 4cm/1½in, **£6–8/$8–13**; miniature "forget-me-not" jug, c.1881–90, ht 3.5cm/1¼in, **£25–30/$40–50**

the "Nottingham Urn" illustrated above centre is, according to the label on the base of the piece, now in the town's Castle Museum. The inscription does not always make a piece more valuable, as shown by the miniature forget-me-not jug, which is not a named model but is worth more.

The graceful limpet shell on orange coral legs, right, belongs to the group of Goss shapes that have no specific matching crest. Those models with a link to a particular area, such as an "Abergavenny Jar", will have double or treble the normal value if they have the matching place-name crest. Originally each shape was linked with one town or village in particular, but when agencies became tired of stocking the same old shapes they appealed to the Goss factory for a greater variety on which to emblazon their crest. The range of shapes available was extended to include buildings, animals, fonts, and miniature tea sets so tiny and delicate they were hard to pick up.

The onset of World War I meant that the demand for Goss china diminished, marking the end of the craze with which the nation had for so long been besotted. The Goss factory was sold in 1929, and some of the last crested pieces to be made by the new owner were for the 1938 Scottish Empire Exhibition in Glasgow.

As heraldic ware fell out of favour, crested china was thrown away and now, sadly, though probably most homes contained crested china during the collecting obsession, less than ten per cent of all the Goss china made survives today.

Limpet shell, c.1890–1929, ht 3.5cm/1¼in **£18–22/$28–35**

Goss cottages

In 1893 Adolphus Goss introduced a new range of seven nightlight cottages that were exact reproductions of famous homes – realistically coloured, and with precise attention to detail. The open back of each piece held a nightlight; when this was lit, smoke came out of the chimneys and the extra-thin porcelain windows glowed in the dark. Instantly successful, the range was extended to 35 cottages. Most of these have survived very well as they are strong and difficult to damage, but some may be restored, with missing chimneys and chipped corners expertly repaired, so check any potential purchases carefully for hidden damage. The two most common models are Ann Hathaway's cottage and Shakespeare's birthplace in Stratford-upon-Avon. Today the rarest and most valuable British ones are the plainest, as fewer were made.

The Tudor house from Southampton, c.1893–1929, ht 8.5cm/3½in, **£330–350/ $530–560**

▲ The Tudor house

Possibly the most attractive cottage is the timbered Tudor house from Southampton, shown above. The original is still standing in Bugle Street and is now a museum, with a Goss model of itself as one of the exhibits. The inscription on the base of this cottage associates the building with royal visits by Henry VIII, Anne Boleyn and Philip II of Spain.

▼ Famous homes

The cottages selected by Goss included those associated with famous people from history. The lexicographer Dr Johnson was born in this house at Lichfield. The Goss cottages were made over a period of 40 years, and although there is fairly good consistency across this time there are sometimes slight differences in the depth of colour and detail in identical models. Moulds had to be replaced after several weeks of use, and this contributed to slight size differences. Some cottages were glazed, which appears to intensify the colours, but most are found unglazed.

Dr Samuel Johnson's house, Lichfield, c.1912–29, ht 7.5cm/3in, **£180–200/ $290–320**

- The "Old Toll Bar, Gretna Green" is one of few cottages with no factory mark, but this does not affect its high value of £2,200/$3,520 (if perfect).
- Most cottages are worth £20/$32 extra if glazed.
- English cottages dated post-1929, when the Goss factory was sold, are worth less than the pre-1929 models.

Charles Dickens' house at Gads Hill, Rochester, c.1914–29, ht 6.5cm/2½in, **£150–180/$240–290**

▲ **Charles Dickens' house**
When it was discovered, owing to ivy being cut away from the walls, that the original house had porch windows, the Goss factory remodelled its piece in keeping with its strict rule on accuracy. This later, amended version is the one shown above. However, it is the earlier version, without porch windows, that is the rarer model, and this adds £50/$80 to the value.

▼ **Variety**
Thatched cottages such as the "Old Maids' Cottage" at Lee, have painstaking detail in the paned windows and rambling ivy. These models differ greatly to the white, named buildings, mostly of the second period of 1881–1934, such as the "Grinlow Tower". Occasionally reject white-glazed cottages appear with a Blackpool crest, such as the "Abbot's Kitchen"; though rare they are worth much less.

"Old Maids' Cottage", c.1913–29, l. 7.5cm/3in, **£130–145/$210–230**

St Nicholas' Chapel, Ilfracombe, c.1913–29, l. 7.5cm/3in, **£150–170/$240–270**

▲ **Devon & Cornwall pieces**
Churches and chapels were popular subjects to be replicated in china. Devon and Cornwall, in southern England, were favourite places with Adolphus Goss, and he selected this chapel at Ilfracombe, Devon, and the St Nicholas chapel at St Ives, Cornwall. Two oddities to look out for in this range are the "Huers House" and the "Look-out House" with its portholes, both realistic and recognizable models of houses on the coast at Newquay in Cornwall.

Arcadian

Arcadian ware is not translucent like Goss or Grafton, or as immaculate as Carlton (see pp.16–17), but it is well produced and covers a vast range of pieces. The company copied Goss with its artefacts and historical shapes, before progressing to realistic and splendid animals and birds, buildings, monuments, historical shapes such as the "Leominster Ducking Stool" and national souvenirs like the "Ripon Hornblower". The "Great War" range is probably the best, with soldiers and sailors, tanks, guns, ships, bombs and, after 1918, war memorials. Arcadian's largest range is called "Home Nostalgic" and includes coal buckets, pillar boxes, miniature teapots with lids, sundials and fireplaces. More Arcadian crested china was made than any other make, and it was sold in every possible outlet – all through the entrepreneurial ambitions of its founder, Harold Taylor Robinson.

Acorn, c.1903–33,
ht 5.5cm/2⅛in,
£8–12/$13–20

▶ **Unusual Crests**
Arcadian managed to obtain orders for items showing the crests of the tiniest villages and remotest outposts. This Arcadian acorn has the arms of the small village of Wool, in Dorset. If there was not already a registered coat-of-arms for a particular village, then Arcadian designed one. Some remote places had only a few pieces made for them, and these rare pieces are worth keeping for future investment.

▼ **Bottles**
Arcadian's bottles were made in two different sizes. The larger size is illustrated below and came either with a solid top or with a cork, as shown here. Despite these variations, all versions of the bottles seem to be worth more or less the same amount. There are also variations with the names. Many of the bottles are not named at all, but if they are titled it is usually "One Special Scotch", "One Special Irish" or, more rarely, "Lacon's Fine Ale". These inscriptions add £4–5/$6.50–8 to the value of a bottle.

"One Special Scotch" bottle,
c.1903–33, ht 7.5cm/3in,
£8–10/$13–16

▼ Subsidiary manufacturers of Arcadian

Largely owing to Harold Taylor Robinson's ambitions, Arcadian was the owner of more than 40 other potteries that also made crested china. These included Swan, Botolph, Coronet Ware, Griffin China and Robinson & Leadbeater, the latter making an excellent range of parian busts. Also part of the group was Wembley China, which was the trademark used on the Wembley-crested Arcadian shapes at the British Empire Exhibition of 1924 and 1925. Any item carrying this crest is worth more than those with other town arms. The charabanc pictured below was made by several different potteries, all of which were owned by Arcadian.

Charabanc, c.1903–33,
l. 14cm/5½in, **£40–50/$65–80**

Manx cat, c.1903–33,
l. 7cm/2¾in, **£35–40/$55–65**

▲ Manx cat

Arcadian produced the widest range of animals, including this Manx cat. Any agency could order this cat with its own crest but few did because the Manx cat is such an unusual animal. How the Manx cat itself actually evolved is a mystery; Joseph Turner, the great English artist, claimed to own seven of these creatures. Today large numbers of Manx cats have found homes in the USA, and their crested china replicas can be found there too.

▼ Arcadian marketing

The Goss factory concentrated on the same sober and traditional styles, while other firms exploited the ever-growing market. Arcadian captured everyday life with items such as this basket of "gold-tops", below, which was how milk used to be delivered. Arcadian's "Miniature Series" catalogue promised: "Goods sent carriage forward. Packages charged for and credited in full on return. Discounts 3¾% – 7 days; 2½% – 30 days, afterwards nett."

Basket of gold-top milk bottles, c.1903–33, ht 6.5cm/2½in, **£18–25/$28–40**

Black cats & black boys

After World War I there was a craze for "lucky" souvenirs, from lucky black-cat transfers on china featuring horseshoes and swastikas (which, pre-WWII, were good luck symbols) to black boys. Cats are renowned for having nine lives, and black ones are linked with magic and witchcraft and are generally believed to bring good luck. All this was not lost on Arcadian's Harold Taylor Robinson, and his lucky black cats became a best-selling line. After 1925 Arcadian and Willow Art both brought out a daring range of black boys – an intolerable concept today. Black boys and girls were an innovative line in the craze for "enchanting children", and more black child figures were made than those with blonde hair and rosy cheeks. Despite the larger number, the black child figures still command the higher prices.

▼ Registered series
This cat model is one of a series of 24 that was registered in 1924: the later the number, the more intricate the model, and therefore the more expensive. The cats had one yellow eye, one green eye and red or yellow bows. At number 21, the "Cats on a Seesaw", was at the top end of the pricing scale, and therefore not many exist today. Another rarity is five cats on the roof of a house, their tails dangling down to spell "LUCK".

Arcadian "Cats on a Seesaw", c.1925, l. 8.5cm/3⅓in, **£180–200/ $290–320**

► Nursery rhymes
Number 12, "Black Cat in Well", is possibly derived from the English nursery rhyme *Ding Dong Bell, Pussy's in the Well*; the seesaw piece could also originate from a nursery rhyme. Cats were often shown adopting sporting poses, such as riding a scooter or bicycle, sailing a yacht or paddling a canoe, and one piece has three cats riding a sledge down a hill. Other themes are musical, including cats playing a piano and a double bass. There are also the "action" cats: operating a radio, talking on the telephone, sitting on a swing or posting a letter in a pillar box.

Arcadian "Black Cat in Well", c.1924–39, ht 6.5cm/2½in, **£60–65/ $95–105**

• "Black Felix the Cat" is shown walking on various different items and today fetches at least £150/$240.
• Carlton made a black girl in a hip bath of black water captioned "I'se making Ink", now worth £90–100/$145–160.
• Many "Black Boys" were made as salt and pepper pots.

▼ **Domesticated cats**

The more domesticated cats are depicted peeping out of an old boot, curled up in a pram, grouped together in a bed, lying on a brick wall and also sitting on a vertical horseshoe for double luck. In 1925 Arcadian published a catalogue of its stock, and these cats were the only items to be featured in colour. The cheapest cats were sold to the agencies for 12 shillings (60p/95cents) per dozen, and the most expensive cost 18 shillings (90p/$1.45) for twelve.

Arcadian "Black Cat in Old Boot", c.1924–33, ht 6cm/2¼in, **£70–75/$110–120**

▼ **Black boys**

Like the cats, these boys (and sometimes girls) are given occupations, such as eating a slice of melon, playing the banjo or being chased by a crocodile. One piece shows a black boy sitting up in bed with hand-painted brown or black spiders on the bedclothes, captioned "Just a little study in black and fright". The boy is usually wearing red, blue or yellow striped pyjamas with a yellow belt. It is unbelievable in today's society that these figures, with such titles, were made, but in the mid-1920s they were very popular. The principal factories of Shelley, Willow and Arcadian all made their own versions.

Arcadian "Black Boy eating Melon", c.1925–33, ht 7cm/2¾in, **£140–160/$225–255**

Arcadian "Black Cat in Old Boot", c.1924–33, ht 6cm/2¼in, £70–75/$110–120

Arcadian "Black Baby eating Boiled Egg", c.1925–33, ht 7cm/2¾in, **£140–160/$225–255**

▲ **Expressions**

The expressions on faces were governed by the positioning of the white eyes and the droop of the red lips. For example, black boys in a scrape, like the one peeping out naked from behind a shower, have their mouths turned down at the corners. The boy above, with his boiled egg hatching, has a round open mouth to show surprise.

Carlton

James F. Wiltshaw and Harold Taylor Robinson (later of Arcadian) began manufacturing Carlton ware in 1890, but it was not until 1902 that they advertised their heraldic china. Unlike many other potteries that were eventually taken over, Carlton stayed independent, with Wiltshaw as sole proprietor by 1911. Like the Goss factory, Carlton insisted that only the correct version of a town's coat-of-arms be used. Its range is consistently fine and of excellent quality, and was altered to suit the public mood, from "flappers" to busts of John Bull, from radio operators to domestic ware. The firm could not fight the depression in the potting industry, and in 1931 went into receivership, but after merging with Savoy China, Carlton was able to continue production of crested ware for a couple of years.

◀ **Designs**
From 1924 onwards Carlton used five shades of lustre on the finish of its wares, known as "lustrine", such as the sailing yacht illustrated left with its mother-of-pearl lustre. The four other lustre colours are orange, yellow, turquoise and pink. The firm was at the height of its crested china production, and Wiltshaw was keen to produce unique in-house designs. Few transfers were made, but those that do exist are well defined. Pieces decorated with forget-me-nots, shamrocks and bouquets of roses are highly sought after.

"Saucy Sue" sailing yacht, c.1924, l. 11cm/4¼in, **£30–35/ $50–55**

▼ **Keeping warm**
Certain shapes were made only by Carlton, Swan and Arcadian, including the "Old Warming Pan" below, which is usually labelled "Sally warm the bed" or, as here, "Polly warm the bed" (referring to the maid). This was a Swan mould, bought by Carlton but taken to Arcadian when Robinson left the company. There was no central heating in the early 20thC, and many everyday heating items, such as ranges, fireplaces, bellows, coal hods and scuttles, sacks of coal and even a pair of blankets, were reproduced as crested china souvenirs.

"Old Warming Pan", c.1902–30, l. 12.5cm/ 5in, **£16–20/ $26–30**

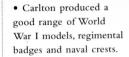

▼ World War I

Carlton issued the largest fleet of WWI battleships, with over 30 different varieties and names. Below is HMS *Lion*, which has three funnels and four guns fore, two guns amidships and two aft. Other battleships came with two funnels or two guns fore and aft. As well as a range of smaller, wider battleships with and without guns, there is an unusual one with both bow and stern rolled inwards. "HMS *Humber*" (also known as "Model of British Monitor") has a high prow and is a rare piece. Another particularly scarce ship has a pinnacle with a strange bulbous base instead of the more usual funnel.

HMS *Lion* battleship, c.1902–30, ht 11.5cm/4½in, **£90–110/ $145–175**

Windmill with revolving sails, c.1902–30, ht 10.5cm/4½in, **£40–50/$65–80**

▲ Buildings of yesteryear

Windmills were still in use in Edwardian times. Carlton made the loveliest examples, with separate revolving sails connected with fuse wire. Most unusual white-glazed buildings were issued: the rare model of a pithead with its pulley and moulded ropes; the "Beacon" at Alderley Edge; and "Martello Tower" inscribed "The Martello Wish Tower, erected in 1804, the date of Napoleon's threatened invasion".

"Map of Blighty", c.1902–30, ht 11.5cm/4½in, **£75–85/$120–135**

▲ Patriotic pieces

The World War I pieces made by Carlton were heavy with patriotism, and none more so than this "Map of Blighty" with five lines of the poem *Take me back to dear old Blighty* on it. Another popular piece in the range was the traditional "John Bull with his Bulldog" figurine on an oval base, trimmed with the colours of the Union Jack, which is now worth £195/$310.

Shelley

In 1883 the Foley China Works at Longton, Staffordshire, was run by the Shelley family. As there were already several Foley works in the Longton area the name was changed to Shelley in 1910, but many Shelley models, especially animals, are actually marked Foley, not Shelley. The company is known for its superb range of teaware – especially the Art Deco designs – and was the only firm to institute a serious stock-numbering system on its models. From 1906 Shelley concentrated on producing a range of beautiful artefacts, buildings, WWI memorabilia, animals and novelty items. Less adventurous in their use of colours, more predictable with their interpretations of models and more likely to use realistic rather than idealistic shapes, Shelley pieces appeal to a large group of enthusiastic collectors.

▼ Fun furniture

Shelley made a wonderfully original range of souvenirs reproducing everyday household implements and even furniture. The roll-topped desk, for example, was something not attempted by other potteries, as was the swing mirror on a stand, with silvered glass. The upright piano shown here, with its sheet music, pedals and open, painted keyboard, is particularly rich in detail.

Piano no. 345,
c.1903–23,
ht 7.5cm/3in,
£35–40/
$55–65

▶ Crested time

Many factories produced mantel, grandfather and grandmother clocks; Arcadian made an alarm clock, and Corona offered a fob watch. The most elegant clock, however, was the Shelley longcase version, which was named with a range of titles such as "Burns Clock" or "Model of 14th Century Clock in Wallace Collection". The particular shape pictured right can also be found labelled "Wake up and Get to Business", or even "The Moving Finger Writes and having Writ Moves On". The latter inscription is the most scarce and is worth an extra £10/$16.

"BURNS"
GRANDFATHER
CLOCK

Grandfather
clock no. 307,
c.1903–23,
ht 13cm/5in,
£18–20/
$28–30

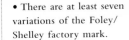

▼ Novelty items

Shelley had a small comic, or novelty, line, and none of these items was at all controversial with the uncomfortable exception of this little "black boy" with his hands gripping the edge of the bath labelled "How Ink Is Made". Shelley's real forte was its amazing animals, unusual World War I artefacts and "home nostalgic" shapes. Its animals are mainly realistic, but there are a few surprises: the scarce and comical "Pup", with black ears and spots, is enormous and has an appealing stance, while a "Pig" sitting upright with folded arms can be found, inscribed "Very Umble". However, the strangest Shelley animal is the "Penguin", which has a black beak and is holding a folded newspaper under one wing.

"Black Boy in Bath" no. 374, c.1903–23, l. 11cm/4¼in, **£90–110/$145–175**

▼ Seaside speciality

The seaside was a Shelley speciality – if other potteries produced souvenirs of simple bathing machines, the Shelley example was superlative. The "Life Saver", below, was made by Saxony as well, but its version is a poor figure in comparison. The "Paddle Steamer" is magnificent, while lighthouses, fish baskets and life belts are complemented with whelk, scallop and winkle shells, plus a Lyme Regis ammonite.

"Life Saver" no. 410, c.1903–23, ht 11cm/4¼in, **£70–80/ $110–130**

- There are at least seven variations of the Foley/ Shelley factory mark.
- The range of numbered ancient artefacts could well increase in value, but they are currently selling for £5/$8 plus.
- Animals and WWI items were Shelley's best lines. A Shelley animal is worth more than its equal from most other potteries.

▼ Transport

The model cars made by Shelley are exotic, detailed models of the more expensive makes on the market. Cars had only been invented at the end of the 19thC – the new-fangled contraption had changed people's lives forever, so these were exciting times to be living in. Shelley's "Motor Coupé" had a folded-down hood, buttoned-down upholstery and raised lamps. The "Charabanc" is labelled "The Monarch", for unknown reasons, while later models of the "Vauxhall Staff Car" are considered WWI pieces.

"Vauxhall Staff Car" no. 361, c.1903–23, l. 13.5cm/5¼in **£140–160/$225–255**

HOW INK IS MADE

Willow Art

Edwin Leadbeater and his brother-in-law Arthur Hewitt owned the second most prolific firm to make crested china, produced from 1905 onwards. The range of coloured cottages was more varied than that of Goss (see pp.10–11), and the white-glazed ware was of excellent quality. Few transfers were produced, and the firm concentrated on its vast range of shapes, culminating in 1922 with the comical cartoon characters "Mr Beetle" and "Teddy Tail". A splendid Willow figure is the "Drunk", in top hat and tails, draped around a female statue inscribed "How cold you are tonight". In 1925 Robinson of Arcadian acquired Willow Art, and from then onwards the firm is remembered for its superb range of buildings, statues and transport pieces, including double-decker and single-decker trams, charabancs and open-top sports cars.

▼ **Choice subjects**
Willow was adept at choosing a subject that represented a particular town or area, like this "River Thames Pleasure Punt": even its gaily-painted plush cushions match the colours of the Windsor crest. Other Willow subjects are the "Reading Biscuit", "Melton Mowbray Pie" (complete with lattice pastry adornments), "Banbury Cake", "Bolton Trotter" (a pig's foot) and "Yarmouth Bloater", all named after towns in England. "Daniel Lambert of Leicester", modelled sitting in a vast chair, was the fattest man in England.

"River Thames Pleasure Punt", c.1905–30, l. 17.5cm/7in, **£140–160/ $225–255**

"Old Maids' Cottage" at Lee, c.1905–30, l. 6cm/2¼in, **£55–65/ $90–105**

▲ **Old Maids' Cottage**
Two Willow versions exist of this cottage, one with a brown thatched roof, as here, and one with a yellow. Both are cruder than the Goss model (see p.11), but are gaily coloured, with painted leaded windows. The three young women who lived there were known as "the old maids of Lee" because of their fussiness in choosing husbands.

"Lady Godiva Coventry",
c.1905–30, ht 8cm/3¼in,
£60–70/$95–110

▲ **Lady Godiva**
Coventry is still famous for this legend: in 1040 Lady Godiva, the wife of the Earl of Mercia, protested against her husband's high taxes on the people of the city, and to persuade him to lower them she rode naked on horseback through the town. All shielded their eyes apart from one man, who became known as "Peeping Tom" – also immortalized in crested china. Godiva's aged husband died some years later, in 1057, and she then took control of the taxes herself. The Goss coloured busts of "Peeping Tom" and "Lady Godiva" are highly collectable, as is this parian figure of her riding naked on her horse.

▼ **Pillar boxes**
The ubiquitous pillar box, such as this Willow one with a verse on the back – "If you haven't got time to post a line here's the pillar box" – was the ideal gift to give to someone you would like to hear from more often. Superior to the Florentine, the Gemma and even the Arcadian version, the Willow also comes in a giant size. Less important makers produced post boxes with no open slots, the verse on the top or no verse at all, and the crest on the upright. Stamp boxes were also made, to become part of a stamp enthusiast's collection – indeed collecting crested china was three-dimensional stamp collecting.

Pillar box with George V monogram, c.1911–30, ht 9cm/3½in, **£25–30/$40–50**

Fat lady on scales,
c.1920–30, ht 9cm/3½in,
£75–85/$120–135

▲ **Comical crested ware**
Willow produced various comic items like this "fat lady" figure above: a broad bean pod saying "Good Old Bean"; a series of three eggs, with a yellow chick, a flapper's blonde head and a black boy hatching from them; "Winkie the Glad Eyes Bird" with one eye winking; "Mr Pickwick", a drunk, bald little man in green climbing up an assortment of bottles and beakers; and "Sunny Jim", a 1920s cartoon character.

Savoy & other major potteries

Savoy china was produced by Birks, Rawlins & Co. at the Vine Pottery in Stoke. From 1910 the firm produced seaside ware, a large range of animals, cartoon characters and musical instruments, but its forte was the World War I range. The biplanes, with coloured roundels and tail fins, are breathtaking. Savoy also made a series of miniatures carrying over 60 commemorative battle inscriptions with exact dates and locations. These are becoming very collectable and sell today for £10–20/$16–30 each. There are over 360 different English factory marks recorded on crested china, and some factories have several versions of these. Companies that made a major contribution to the crested china industry include Grafton, Wilton, Podmore, Florentine, Corona and Alexandra.

▼ Fireplaces

When this piece was made, c.1919–21, fireplaces like this would have been found in many homes. The mantel cloth, clock and china ornaments were all common everyday things. Kettles were heated up over coal fires, and teapots were left warming by grates. The china models usually came with the verse "East or West, Home is Best, Home Sweet Home".

Brick fireplaces can sometimes double up as "home nostalgic" items (see p.50) and as WWI pieces (see pp.36–41) when the verse is changed to "We've Kept the Home Fires Burning".

Sylvan kitchen range, c.1919–21, ht 9.5cm/3¾in, **£25–30/$40–50**

▶ Plymouth

Plymouth was a natural focus for crested china manufacturers as it had so many local landmarks. Devonia Art, a subsidiary of Willow Art, produced "Derry's Clock Tower", the "Armada Memorial", "Drake Statue", "Mayflower Stone", "Plymouth War Memorial" (with angel), "Naval War Memorial" and "Citadel Gateway", seen here by Grafton. The Plymouth agency W. B. was particularly successful and kept Devonia Art busy with supplying stock. As Plymouth is a naval base there is a large selection of WWI models displaying the crests of Plymouth and nearby Stonehouse.

Grafton "Citadel Gateway", Plymouth, c.1915–33, ht 12cm/4¾in, **£45–50/$70–80**

▼ Artefacts

Most small pieces are not named, but those that do carry inscriptions on the bases are known as named models or artefacts. Just about any one of 7,000 known crests and decorations can appear on these pots, or transfers like this rather gruesome "Scold's Bridle" (used by men in the middle ages to stop women nagging). Carlton, Savoy, Grafton and Shelley made some very fine artefacts, and they all attempted to number their wares. The original versions are in museums nationwide, and many have social and historical relevance.

Savoy handled tyg showing "The Scold's Bridle", c.1910–33, ht 6cm/2¼in **£15–20/$25–30**

Savoy golf ball, c.1910–33, ht 4.5cm/1¾in, **£15–20/$25–30**

▲ Golfing memorabilia

Golf is a very popular game today, but 100 years ago only those few people fortunate enough to afford it could play, as was the case with so many elitist sports at the start of the last century. Golf balls and golf-club heads named "Fore" were produced, as were golfers wearing plus fours and peaked caps, bent over their putts on ashtray bases. A very rare unmarked example in beige has occasionally been seen, and this could now be worth around £200–300/$320–480.

Wedgwood, Worcester and Royal Doulton produced so few crested pieces (mainly vases) that they are now worth up to five times more than those by other makers. Any crested item by Belleek is worth as much as £100/$160, but Grafton is possibly the finest of the potteries to make crested ware.

▼ The Gynn Inn

Blackpool's Gynn Inn was a much-loved British landmark. Situated on the beach, it saved a Scottish schooner from shipwreck during a summer storm in 1833 by guiding it to safety with a lantern hung in an upstairs window. In 1900, when the promenade was extended to create the promenade tramway, the Gynn Inn was demolished, causing a public outcry. The Grafton factory responded with its model so that the local landmark would live on.

Grafton "Gynn Inn", c.1906–33, l. 12.5cm/5in, **£130–150/ $210–240**

German souvenir ware

Throughout the latter half of Queen Victoria's reign German potteries supplied British seaside towns with cups, saucers, plates, jugs, bowls and teapots, often painted bright pink and known as German souvenir ware. The greyish china was bisque rather than parian ware and came from central Germany (Saxony, Bavaria and Thuringia) as well as Austria, Poland and Carlsbad in Czechoslovakia. These potteries were unable to ship goods to Britain during World War I, and after the war they struggled to secure orders with anti-German British retailers. However, they got round this by marking their wares as made in Austria or Czechoslovakia, or simply as "Foreign".

German bathing belle with parasol, c.1920–39, ht 12cm/4¾in, **£25–30/$40–50**

▶ Bathing belles

The Germans were quick to note that the public were taken with "bathing belle" figures in any shape or form, such as sunbathing on the edge of a shell, peeping out of a changing tent or leaning on a globe of the world. They appealed to the lower end of the market, the "bazaar trade" as it was known, and some consider these figures, often in a yellow/brown wash, as vulgar. Other models in the range include "bell hops" (hotel porters) on suitcases and luggage trolleys, and children on swings and slides. These figures were often made in pairs – a boy and a girl.

▼ Mosanic buildings

This range was made before WWI by Max Emmanuel & Co. in Bavaria. The buildings are mostly unglazed and drab brown in colour, to look like stone, but show great attention to detail. Very few carry heraldic devices. They usually have registration numbers of four figures impressed on the bases, as well as stock numbers. So far 80 have been recorded, most retailing now at between £30/$50 and £40/$65.

Mosanic St Paul's Cathedral, London, c.1920–39, l. 9cm/ 3½in, **£30–35/$50–55**

Parrot eating berries,
c.1920–39, ht 6.5cm/2½in,
£14–18/$22–28

▲ Fairings

This gaily coloured parrot eating red berries has no heraldic crest. The Germans realised that the appeal of the crests was dwindling and led the move towards fairings – garish, brightly coloured souvenirs that said "A Present from ..." or "Souvenir of ...". A series of amusing aeroplanes, a variety of dogs, linked wedding rings, and gnomes, all on small bases, were produced and labelled as "presents". On some the detail is quite intricate, considering that these were aimed at the cheaper end of the market.

▼ Animals

Unlike the Staffordshire-made crested china animals, which were delicate and translucent, with restrained detail, the German offerings were flamboyant and gaudy. This superb snail would probably attract more interest in today's market than its only rival – a Grafton model. Beware of a more recent foreign range of animals, dating from c.1940–50, with ashtray bases and five-figure numbers, which are of poorer quality and have no crests or "A Present from" labels; an example of these later models is a "Duckling", wearing a hat and carrying an umbrella, on a leaf-shaped mauve base impressed with no. 11448. Only collect four-figure numbers.

Snail in lustre, c.1910–39,
l. 11cm/4¼in, **£20–25/$30–40**

German orange-lustre cruet binoculars, c.1910–39, ht 7.5cm/3in, **£10–12/$16–20**

▲ Cruet sets

Many 1930s homes had vulgar coloured-lustre cruets in the shape of an aeroplane, a motor car, lighthouse, steam-ship, an elephant, and so on, and those that were not used daily survive today. There was usually a section for mustard, and hollowed salt and pepper ends with corks and loose tops. The Germans were especially proud of their colour transfers, and used these more than crests as decoration. The biggest market for cruet sets is the USA.

Decorations on crested china

Transfer scenes on crested china offer a good variety of colour – black and sepia, and, more rarely, red, blue or green, were often used on the crested shapes. Scenes of village life were popular, showing trees, houses, ladies in the long skirts of the time, horses and carts and early motor cars. Other decorations include flowers, shamrocks, military badges and naval crests. Of all the potteries, Goss produced the best commemoratives, including royal, regional and military pieces. Sales of transfers dropped dramatically when the picture postcard became the cheaper alternative in 1900. Later models made in the 1920s and 1930s were more brightly coloured, in shades of lustre, and these often now fetch higher prices than earlier, less colourful ones, with the exception of Goss pieces.

▼ **Good-luck transfers**
This Carlton jug has an unusual good-luck decoration, combining an upright horseshoe tied with ribbon, a tiny cat and the words "A Charming Souvenir from Folkestone", as opposed to "A present from ...". The unusual transfer, combined with the blue lustre, makes this jug stand out from the normal ivory-coloured ware. The more usual lucky black-cat transfers are worth £10–20/$16–30 each, but "Felix the Cat" (a cartoon character) transfers fetch more than £50/$80 each. Wilton China issued Felix transfers with a circular design underneath reading "Pathé presents in Eve and Everybodys film Review", referring to a contemporary cinema newsreel.

Carlton blue-lustre jug,
c.1902–30,
ht 5cm/2in,
£18–22/
$30–35

▶ **Scenic transfers**
The best quality transfers are those by Goss, but just as rare are the scenic transfers from other potteries, like this Willow Art castle scene. A series of mainly sepia transfers was made by Goss for the Canadian market; these are exceptionally rare and can fetch at least £100/$160 each. Early polychrome and monochrome views on any Goss shape add an extra £50–70/$80–110, and on any piece of crested china they add £7–15/$11–25, or more if a car or a train is featured.

Willow Art book,
c.1907–25,
ht 5.5cm/2in,
£16–20/
$26–30

Carlton goose on green base, c.1902–30, ht 7cm/2¾in, **£33–36/$53–58**

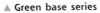

FACT FILE

- Goss military badges are £50/$80 or more each, against £20/$30 or less with most other makers.
- Noble, ecclesiastical, foreign and school crests are two or three times more valuable than town or village coat-of-arms.
- Goss christening mugs and beakers with initials fetch £30–60/$48–95; Q and I are very rare.

▼ Military badges

China carrying the crest of corps and regiments was not sold until the outbreak of WWI, and most was taken out of production when peace was declared. Goss models have the best quality and widest range, but Willow and Arcadian come close. The RFC and RNAS joined forces to form the RAF in April 1918, as shown on the propellers below. The *Goss Record War Edition* (catalogue of pieces) refers to the army regimental badges of Farnborough and Eastbourne, featured here: "The soldiers themselves have taken the keenest delight in obtaining the charming little models bearing their regimental arms and sending them to friends and relatives as keepsakes."

Unmarked Willow Art aeroplane propellers, c.1914–25, l. 15cm/6in, **£80–85/$130–135 (each)**

▲ Green base series

Carlton produced a series of five birds, all with yellow beaks, perched on green bases, including the goose pictured above. The other four birds are a cockerel with an ornate tail, pecking the ground; a large duck standing upright in a comical pose; a duck airing its gilded wings; and a fantail turkey. The birds are rarely found with the beige ground and "Lucky White Heather" message seen on this goose. Rarer still are those coloured red or blue all over.

Swan China vase, c.1904–25, ht 6.5cm/2½in, **£20–22/$30–35**

▲ Motto ware

Various decorations on crested china, including cartoons and enamel pictures by the artist Raphael Tuck, were accompanied by a motto such as "No life can be dreary when work is a delight". A particularly amusing motto is "A handsome shoe often pinches the foot", but this one is a rarity and not easy to find. These mottoes are charming, and their sentiments can still raise a smile today.

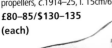

The seaside

Workplaces throughout Britain usually closed down for a week during August, and the entire staff and their families would spend their holiday "wakes week" at the seaside. Margate, Blackpool and Eastbourne were favoured places, and what better souvenir to take home than a crested "Blackpool Wheel", a "Margate Clock Tower" or a pretty whelk shell from Eastbourne. Arcadian and Willow Art produced a selection of seaside souvenirs, from fishing boats to a range of lighthouses, seashells, bathing machines, bandstands and even lifebelts. Carlton's version of the "Punch and Judy Show" is the best of its kind, valued at £100/$160. Busts of "Punch and Judy" also exist, and the third-period Goss "Punch and Judy" cruet set has Toby the dog as the mustard pot – valued at £150/$240 for the set. Seaside china is a popular, fun and varied collecting theme.

▶ New trends

The era between the two world wars saw a distinct trend towards bright, garish colours and Art Deco lines, and a decline of interest in heraldry. The Germans were quick to exploit this, and responded with brightly coloured ranges such as this "flapper" in her gay swimming cap and costume and "modern" heeled shoes, reclining on an angular ashtray. Smoking was another fashion of the time, and some figures were made with flappers smoking cigarettes. There is no crest on this piece; instead it features a colourful transfer of the seaside at Aberystwyth, as transfers were coming back into vogue once again.

Bathing belle on ashtray, no. 2853, by "Foreign" maker, c.1920–39, ht 7.5cm/3in, **£30–40/$50–65**

▼ Realistic rock

The rarest salt and pepper shakers to be made as souvenir china were in the form of a stick of rock (sickly-sweet sugary bars). Bright pink is the most usual colour, with the pink on the outside being picked up by the lettering within the rock. The few examples that have been found so far are souvenirs from the coastal resorts of Southsea, Great Yarmouth and Clacton, but there are certainly more pieces, from other towns, for the dedicated collector to find.

Carlton stick of Clacton rock, c.1902–30, ht 7.5cm/3in, **£100–120/ $160–190**

Willow Art lighthouse,
c.1902–30, ht 10.5cm/4¼in,
£8–10/$13–16

▲ Lighthouses

Most potteries produced basic
lighthouses on rocky bases
as part of their seaside
collection. A lighthouse
lantern was usually a
fire burning in a metal
basket, hence the
grilles at the tops of
the china models. Warnings
were printed on some, such as
"Sailor Beware" on the Carmen
and Carlton pieces. Others were
modelled on actual lighthouses.
Carlton made more than Goss,
producing over 16 different
types including "Mumbles",
"Chapman" and "Flamborough".

▼ Models from the sea

The various seaside souvenirs
include a delicate and varied
range of seashells, lobster pots
(by Goss for the Channel Islands
of Sark, Guernsey, Jersey and
Alderney), fish baskets (some
with lids), crabs, lobsters and
even a Willow Art mermaid
seated on a rock combing her
hair. The German version of
the lobster is flaming orange,
sometimes doubling up as a
pin box and lid, and is always
a "present" from somewhere.
Another "Foreign" model is
the lobster catcher with his
net, sitting on a huge lobster.

Willow Art whelk shell,
c.1905–30, l. 11cm/4¼in,
£6–8/$10–13

- Goss made nine
lighthouses, ranging
from the "Eddystone"
at Plymouth (worth
£30/$50) to "St Mary's,
Whitley Bay" (valued
at £750/$1,200).
- The whelk is the most
common seashell made.
- Willow Art's "Truck
of Sand" is identical to
its "Truck of Coal" but
it is painted yellow and
worth double.
- Various models of
donkeys were made,
but the Carlton "Gee
up Neddy", with a small
child riding the donkey,
is the rarest (£70–80/
$110–$130).

▼ The Edwardian promenade

Picture the seaside of the
1900s, with bathing huts
pulled down to the sea by
horses, the lifeboat nearby,
and the orchestra in the
bandstand playing to ladies
with parasols parading in
their long skirts and gentlemen in their striped blazers
and boaters. The china
bandstand below is inscribed
"O Listen to the Band". Crested
seaside models such as this
serve to capture the
atmosphere of a
bygone age.

Carlton bandstand,
c.1902–30,
ht 8.5cm/3½in,
£35–40/$55–65

Buildings & monuments

Hewitt & Leadbeater of Willow Art were known for their outstanding statues, white-glazed and coloured buildings, and this 190-strong range of pieces helped to establish the firm. Arcadian produced a dozen coloured cottages but was most prolific with its white-glazed buildings and statues, making nearly 120. Shelley made fewer than 20, from the delicate three-sided "Rufus Stone" (£8/$13) to the enormous "Rock of Ages" at Cheddar (£15/$24). Savoy China's output includes the magnificent "Aberystwyth University" at £150/$240. Carlton made about 120 quality cottages and towers. More than 75 unglazed brown-coloured (stone) Mosaic buildings were exported from Bavaria by Max Emmanuel; ten years ago his pieces were virtually ignored but are now included in many collections.

Willow Art statue of Queen Victoria, c.1905–30, ht 16cm/6¼in, **£50–60/ $80–95**

▼ Queen Victoria

The death of Queen Victoria in 1901 led to versions of her statue appearing in towns and cities up and down the country. Surprisingly it was left to Willow Art and Arcadian to model her statue in porcelain; they chose to reproduce the ones in Blackburn and Wakefield and to make two sizes of the more popular Windsor statue, seen here. It is a delicate design, with the arm extended. Few models were made, suggesting that Willow and Arcadian did not expect the statue to be a bestseller. Goss made busts of the queen, wearing a variety of mob caps and crowns, from 1886 onwards, and produced a Diamond Jubilee issue, 1896–7, as a memorial of her 60th year.

▶ Crosses

Most villages had their landmarks and crosses, and some of these were selected for reproduction in china. Depending on the success of the local agent and the number of tourists who visited the area, some models sold better than others. The Hindhead cross, although not in a tourist hot spot, was along the busy Portsmouth to London road, and was one of the most common, and attractive, crosses to be replicated. Made before the end of the 19th century, the Goss crosses are sober but beautiful. Some are extremely rare, as the agencies that sold them were in remote areas of Scotland and Wales, such as St Martin's Cross on the Scottish island of Iona.

Gibbett Cross Hindhead.

Arcadian "Gibbet's Cross, Hindhead", c.1903–33, ht 13.5cm/5¼in, **£10–14/$16–22**

THE FORTH   BRIDGE

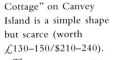

Arcadian Forth Bridge,
c.1903–33, l. 16cm/6¼in,
£40–45/$65–70

▲ **Bridges**
Apart from the third-period
"Clifton Suspension Bridge",
the Goss factory made only
the "Old Gateway" on Monnow
Bridge. "London Bridge",
"Tower Bridge" and "Clifton
Suspension Bridge" were
made by several other
factories. Corona issued a
bridge with grassy banks,
usually showing the crest
of Clacton-on-Sea, which is
probably where the original
can be found. The impressive
Arcadian "Forth Bridge",
pictured above, is a most
ornate and well-made model.

▼ **Towers and castles**
The "King Charles Tower at
Rowton Moor" is so named
because, as inscribed on some
models, King Charles I stood
on this tower in Chester on 24
September 1643 and saw his
army defeated on the moor
below (the battle of Rowton
Heath). Wiltshaw & Robinson
of Carlton made the best and
biggest range of castles and
towers, including the one
pictured, the "Eagle Tower"
and "Douglas Tower of
Refuge". Other towers made
include the "Irish Round",
"Martello", "Old Bishops"
at Paignton, "St Leonards" at
Newton Abbot and "Albert
Memorial Tower" at Belfast.

Carlton "King Charles
Tower at Rowton Moor",
c.1903–33, ht 10.5cm/4¼in,
£35–40/$55–65

Willow Art "Harrogate Pump
House", c.1903–33, ht 7.5cm/3in,
£40–45/$65–70

▲ **Unusual Models**
At least 150 potteries were
competing with ideas and
designs and some unusual
buildings were produced as
a result. The site of Europe's
strongest sulphur well, the
Harrogate Pump Room, was
popular with visitors from all
over the world who came to
drink and bathe in the health-
giving waters, and perhaps
to buy this Willow Art model.

Animals

The most exquisite and elegantly modelled animals are those made by Goss, and these were some of the last models produced in the 1920s. William Henry Goss' grandson John designed most of them, including the "Lion", "Hippopotamus", "Dog" and "Rhinoceros", and they now sell for £300–500/$480–800 each. Over a period of years Grafton offered the widest range of animals and birds (over 140 pieces), while the 70 Arcadian "pets" produced are mostly realistic in appearance. The more complicated models, such as the Grafton "Water Buffalo" (£100/$160), are more valuable, as they were made from several moulds to achieve the complicated shapes. Tuscan made the most exotic animals, of unsurpassable quality, and these are very desirable to collectors. Shelley's animals use the same shapes but with added detail – their "Scottie Dogs" wear black tam o'shanters or pink glengarries.

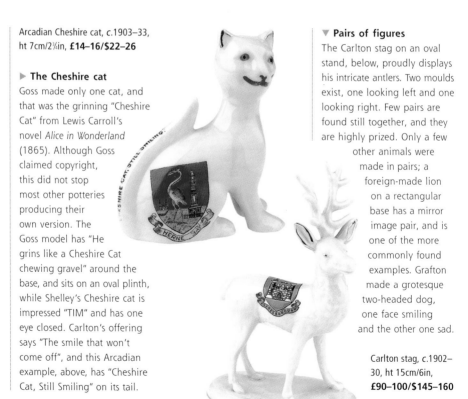

▼ Arcadian Cheshire cat, c.1903–33, ht 7cm/2¾in, **£14–16/$22–26**

▶ **The Cheshire cat**
Goss made only one cat, and that was the grinning "Cheshire Cat" from Lewis Carroll's novel *Alice in Wonderland* (1865). Although Goss claimed copyright, this did not stop most other potteries producing their own version. The Goss model has "He grins like a Cheshire Cat chewing gravel" around the base, and sits on an oval plinth, while Shelley's Cheshire cat is impressed "TIM" and has one eye closed. Carlton's offering says "The smile that won't come off", and this Arcadian example, above, has "Cheshire Cat, Still Smiling" on its tail.

▼ **Pairs of figures**
The Carlton stag on an oval stand, below, proudly displays his intricate antlers. Two moulds exist, one looking left and one looking right. Few pairs are found still together, and they are highly prized. Only a few other animals were made in pairs; a foreign-made lion on a rectangular base has a mirror image pair, and is one of the more commonly found examples. Grafton made a grotesque two-headed dog, one face smiling and the other one sad.

Carlton stag, c.1902–30, ht 15cm/6in, **£90–100/$145–160**

▼ Pigs

The pig was regarded as a good luck symbol during Edwardian times, so many forms and variations of crested china pig were produced by the different potteries. This large range includes Sussex pigs, Hampshire hogs, Wiltshire pigs, long ones, thin ones, fat ones, timid ones, some labelled "I'm the fellow who pays the rent" or "I won't be druv", and some "You can push or you can shuv but I'm hanged if I'll be druv", as well as other stubborn mottoes.

Carlton seated pig,
c.1902–30, ht 9cm/3½in,
£24–28/$40–45

Willow Art collie dog,
c.1905–30, l. 8cm/3¼in,
£20–25/$30–40

▲ Domestic pets

Crested china animals fall into the categories of domestic pet (like the collie above), farmyard, regional, comical, unrealistic and wild animals. The domestic pets were probably easiest to make, and they certainly sold well. There are also many farmyard hens and ducks, but fewer cows, sheep and horses. Welsh mountain goats inscribed "Yr Afr Cymreig" ("The Welsh Goat") come under the regional category (see p.42). Unrealistic pieces include the Cheshire cat on the opposite page and the long-necked cat that was believed to be the mascot on HMS *Lion*.

Grafton baby bird,
c.1915–33, ht 6.5cm/2½in,
£18–22/$28–35

▲ Birds

Arcadian birds are fairly commonplace, but there are not so many made by other manufacturers. This baby bird is quite realistic; Grafton also modelled a kingfisher, a penguin and a very impressive owl. The "Norwich Warbler" often has a whistle inside and a bubble-blower base; the "Norwich Canary" may be painted bright yellow.

Transport

Surprisingly few trains were modelled in porcelain. Carlton produced a copy of "Stephenson's Rocket", labelled "Locomotion 1825", which is now worth £150–175/$240–280, and Shelley made a long locomotive worth a little more than that. Carlton's own version of the long locomotive is equally rare and difficult to find. Saxony's steam locomotive is named "R.H. and D.R." (Romney Hythe and Dymchurch Railway). Coal trucks were more common and often colourful, with the saying "Black Diamonds from ...". The major potteries made a small selection of cars, such as the impressive Shelley "Coupé", the Arcadian "Taxi", the Willow Art "Morris" and the Arcadian two-seater open-top sports car. Carlton also produced a motor scooter, and several of the factories made charabancs (see p.13).

▼ **Motorcycles**

Arcadian, Wembley and Swan China made similar despatch riders on motor-cycles, retailing at about £90–100/$145–160, but only Carlton attempted this intricate motorcyclist-with-sidecar figure. Gemma made a despatch rider's cap with silvered goggles; later versions are considered to be WWI pieces, as the despatch rider was the messenger boy in wartime.

Carlton motor cyclist & side-car, c.1902–30, l. 11cm/4¼in, **£85–100/ $135–160**

▶ **The petrol pump**

Saluting like the early Automobile Association men, this petrol pump attendant has the body of the petrol pump itself. Inscribed "Petrol Sir", the figure recalls the days when petrol pumps were always manned by someone to fill up the tank and take the money. Another tradition that is far less common today is luggage porter trolleys at railway stations. Carlton made a trolley complete with loaded suitcases inscribed "Luggage in Advance" or "LMS RLY to Timbucktoo". A larger foreign version exists, but it does not compare to the Carlton one for quality and delicacy of detail.

Arcadian petrol pump attendant, c.1903–33, ht 9.5cm/3¾in, **£85–95/ $135–150**

• The double-decker
tram is slightly more
valuable than the single-
decker at £200/$320.
• Shelley made a cycle
lamp, worth £70–80/
$110–130.
• A rare piece is the
Shelley "Steamroller",
worth £400–500/
$640–800.
• Rowena's car/ashtray
says "Petrol consumption
nil" and is valued at
£200–250/$320–400.

Florentine motor horn,
c.1913–25, l. 9cm/3½in,
£18–22/$28–35

▲ Motor horns

Crested china has only a few
transport-related items, and the
motor horn above, produced
by Florentine and Coronet
Ware, is one of these. Moulded
in relief on the squeezer end
are the words "Pip Pip". In the
days when roads were rough
and narrow, and there were
still many horses and carts
around, the horn was a vital
piece of equipment. Motor
horns in crested china are
fairly scarce – probably fewer
of these exist than of charabancs and open-top sports
cars. If you look closely at an
Arcadian charabanc you will
see lamps moulded on either
side of the windscreen and
a motor horn fixed to the
right-hand side of the car
(the driver's side in the UK).

Willow Art petrol can,
c.1905–30, ht 5.5cm/2¼in,
£18–20/$28–30

▲ Petrol cans

Several factories made replicas
of petrol cans. The one
featured above has a small
handle and filler cap. During
WWI petrol was not easily
available, so it was a good
idea to carry a can of petrol
in the car. Arcadian and
Willow Art made identical
models to the one illustrated
here. Another version, marked
"Foreign 7214", is much larger
and more detailed but,
as with all German/
Austrian products,
the porcelain is not
as fine. No transport
collection is complete
without a petrol can.

▼ The omnibus & WWI

During the war these public
transport buses, manned by
female drivers and conductors,
carried troops to the front.
Carlton made an excellent job
of reproducing the omnibus
and its driver as well as the
first armoured cars, which
were modified touring cars –
the chassis of makes such as
Rolls-Royce, Talbot, Wolseley
and Lanchester were requisi-
tioned, strengthened, then
armoured and armed.

Carlton double-decker open-top
omnibus, c.1902–30, l. 12.5cm/5in,
£190–200/$305–320

World War I in the air

Aeroplanes were first used in battle during WWI and were made of wood, canvas and wire. The crested china replicas show these details, plus two-, three- or even four-bladed fixed or movable propellers. Earlier models were biplanes, including the "Shelley No. 344", modelled on a Sopwith Scout. Carlton and Savoy both made large detailed biplanes with coloured roundels. Willow Art made the standard monoplane from late 1914; the Arcadian "Model of New Aeroplane" appeared in 1916, probably designed from the Sopwith Pup, and the Shelley 1918 version is derived from a Sopwith Camel. "Super Zeppelins", "British Airships" and the "Beta Balloon" are all quite scarce pieces. Models by Willow Art of an airman standing to attention and an Air Force officer holding his medal are particularly prized, and are both valued at £240–280/$385–450.

▲ Zeppelins

Arcadian "Super Zeppelin", c.1914–33, l. 13cm/5in, **£35–40/ $55–65**

During the war Graf von Zeppelin's airships flew over Belgium, France and Britain dropping their bombs. The Savoy zeppelin was a model of one shot down over Cuffley, Essex, in 1916. This Arcadian example, above, was some-what inaccurate, being modelled on a crashed machine. The Shelley model of 1917 is more realistic. Arcadian made a "Sea-Scout" airship on a stand, known as a "Blimp", in 1915.

▼ Monoplanes

Most of the monoplanes produced by the potteries have some characteristics of the life-size Blériot monoplanes, which were developed after Louis Blériot's flight across the English Channel in 1909. The Willow version came in 1914. Any monoplanes with RFC roundels (discs) can be dated as post-1915; they served as an aid to other pilots to identify the plane as British, rather than German.

Carlton monoplane, c.1902–30, l.14cm/5½in, **£90–100/ $145–160**

- Check if the aeroplane is meant to have a propeller. Revolving propellers are usually fixed with fuse wire.
- Goss produced two bombs and two shells.
- Biplanes had solid or separate double wings – separate is more valuable.
- A Sheringham bomb exists called the "Loftus Bomb", and this is worth another £50/$80 on the usual £250/$400.

▼ Blitzing the zeppelins

This Carlton British searchlight was based on the powerful searchlights that were rigged up to scan the skies at night for the silent zeppelins. Savoy made a model of a vehicle carrying a searchlight, but because it tended to sag the factory issued the faulty range under its Queen's China label. Carlton made a magnificent RNAS motor, and Grafton issued the only airfield tractor driven by a soldier, based on a Holt army tractor used in airfields for towing aeroplanes.

Carlton British searchlight, c.1902–30, ht 7cm/2¾in, **£45–50/$70–80**

Savoy RFC cap, c.1914–33, l. 8cm/3¼in, **£75–85/$120–135**

▲ The pilots

This RFC cap, as reproduced by Savoy, was worn proudly by British pilots. The early pilots were drafted in from cavalry units as it was thought that those who could control horses could also control planes. They were mainly middle and upper-class officers, and in the early days of the war they had to organise and pay for their own pilots' training and licences. However, the ferocious war in the skies took its toll, and these pilots needed replacing at an alarming rate every few weeks. However, life back at base for those who managed to survive was certainly better than for those fighting the war on land.

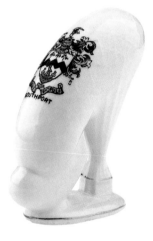

Swan China "Observer Sausage Balloon", c.1914–25, ht 8.5cm/3½in, **£75–80/$120–130**

▲ Balloons

The British Kite Balloon Service was organised to spot artillery. The Observer Sausage Balloons, filled with hydrogen, floated above the trenches on a thin steel cable and collected valuable information for the gunners. They were protected by the men on the ground, but enemy planes could still attack.

World War I at sea

Destroyers, cruisers, minesweepers, torpedo-boat destroyers and converted liners were all depicted in porcelain. Carlton led the way – its range of HMS battleships includes *Canada, Australia, Renown, Iron Duke, Marlborough, Princess Royal* and *Queen Elizabeth*. Savoy also made an impressive fleet of ships including *Barham*. Goss issued a now much sought after contact mine, Shelley a German torpedo head, and Carlton a floating observation mine. There is also a range of sailor figures and busts. Arcadian made a standing sailor, hands on hips, and in 1915 issued a standing sailor winding a capstan (a drum for hauling in rope), which is now much rarer. Grafton made a match-holder in the shape of the head of a German officer peeping out of a lifebelt, now worth £40–50/$65-$80.

▼ **Medical Help**
The Carlton HMHS *Anglia* can be found with the detailed inscription "Model of British Hospital Ship whose voyage was disregarded on three occasions by the German Submarines". The Red Cross and St John's Ambulance Brigade also sent out detachments of ambulances to the front line, with doctors and nurses who daily risked their lives in the war zones. Some very detailed models of nurses and ambulances were produced, but none of doctors.

Carlton
HMHS *Anglia*,
c.1914–20, l.
16.5cm/6½in,
**£150–175/
$240–280**

▲ **Minesweeping**
In 1909 steam fishing trawlers were adapted for minesweeping duties. Captains and volunteers from fishing fleets took on this dangerous job, forming a section of the Royal Naval Reserve. Minesweepers swept in pairs, dragging a weighted cable. When this caught the anchor rope of a mine it was dragged along until the mine exploded. Unexploded mines floated to the surface, to be dealt with later.

Carlton British
minesweeper,
c.1914–18,
l. 11.5cm/4½in,
**£80–85/
$130–135**

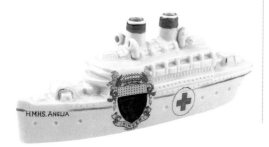

H.M.H.S. ANGLIA

Willow Art "Chatham Naval War Memorial", c.1918–30, ht 16cm/ 6¼in, **£180–200/$290–320**

▲ War memorials

Peace was finally declared in November 1918. The government commissioned Sir Edwin Lutyens to design a symbolic monument to all those who had sacrificed their lives, and the Cenotaph was unveiled in 1920. All over Britain villages and towns designed and built their own tributes, and the potteries modelled many of these as tokens of respect – they were not expected to sell in great numbers. Some of these memorial models are quite rare, but the "Cenotaph" variations are only worth about £10/$16.

▼ Sailor figures & busts

This Arcadian sailor bust can be found with the hat tilted to the left or to the right. The hatband can be named either HMS *Queen Elizabeth* or HMS *Dreadnought*, as here, and the shoulders labelled "The Handyman". Other sailor figures, by Grafton and Wilton, are depicted sitting cross-legged and holding miniature submarines, and are inscribed "We've got 'U' well in hand". A rare fully coloured version can be found, which is worth £200/$320.

Arcadian bust of a soldier, c.1914–20, ht 9cm/3½in, **£45–50/$70–80**

▼ Submarine "E.9."

German U-boats (submarines) kept up a blockade of British ports during the war, sinking supplies from all over the world, including the USA. This caused much anti-German feeling and played an important part in the USA's entry into the war. In 1915 a torpedo sank the RMS *Lusitania* with great loss of life. The ship was modelled by both Carlton and Corona. Britain's answer to the U-boat was the submarine. This Carlton "E.9." is a model of the first submarine to score a direct hit in 1914, succeeding in sinking a German torpedo-boat destroyer.

Carlton "E.9." submarine, c.1914–18, l. 14.5cm/5¾in, **£65–75/$105–120**

World War I on land

When the British "Mark I" tank made its début in the war in 1916 it was immediately copied by crested china potteries and these pieces were seized on by collectors. When a tank featured in the *Daily Mirror* newspaper Arcadian copied it, even if the picture showed it as blown up and without a wheel. (Arcadian then quickly remodelled the tank with two wheels, so the one-wheeled version is now the most sought after). Early armoured cars were modified from fast touring cars, such as the Savoy "Talbot" model (£150–170/ $240–270). Carlton produced excellent likenesses of the anti-aircraft motor, the Rolls-Royce armoured car and the Red Cross van. Uniformed generals were recreated as parian busts, and various china action models of "Tommy" (British soldiers) were made, as well as Scottish soldiers, nurses, bugler boys and a munitions worker carrying shells, all bought by a patriotic public.

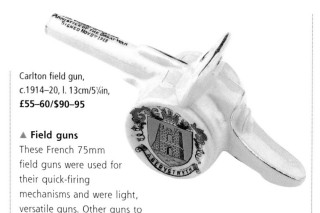

Carlton field gun,
c.1914–20, l. 13cm/5¼in,
£55–60/$90–95

▲ Field guns
These French 75mm field guns were used for their quick-firing mechanisms and were light, versatile guns. Other guns to be produced in crested china included the Arcadian and Swan China field guns with screens and sight holes, various howitzers, and the Grafton "Desert Gun", mounted on a carriage. The Savoy "Trench Mortar" was in fact based on a German gun. One of the rarer guns is the Savoy howitzer with fish tail.

Carlton "HMLS Crème-de-Menthe" tank, c.1914–20, l. 13cm/5¼in, **£40–45/$65–70**

▼ Military tanks
The early tanks underwent trials in 1916 and proved vital to British successes in the war. The "Mark IV" appeared in 1917, minus a steering wheel as army chiefs concluded that wheels were a disadvantage. In 1918 the more versatile "Mark V" was made in two types: a "female" with five machine guns and a "male" with three machine guns and two naval guns. Below is the "Mark IV" tank, named "Crème-de-Menthe" after a battle tank of 1916.

Arcadian "To Berlin",
c.1914–20, l. 12cm/4¾in,
£500–550/$800–880

▼ Mills hand grenade

The original Mills bomb was the principal hand-thrown bomb to be used by the British and was patented by William Mills of Birmingham in 1915. The Shelley one, pictured below, is named as a "Mills Hand Grenade". The Grafton equivalent had a realistic separate metal pin inserted in the top, while the Arcadian version is much smaller and plainer. Other crested grenades were the trench "flying pig", the "plum pudding" bomb and the trench mortar bomb.

Shelley "No. 334 Mills Hand Grenade", c.1914–20, ht 8cm/3¼in,
£25–30/$40–50

▲ "To Berlin"

This amazing figure by Arcadian was never registered as an official model. It may have been issued towards the end of the war when there was less fear that it would be copied by rivals. It also signifies that the allies were on the advance when it was made – chasing and defeating the enemy. The "Tommy" figure was also depicted as a British cavalry officer riding horseback, a "Tommy Atkins the Territorial Officer" bust, a standing drummer boy, a bugler boy, a Grafton bomb thrower and climbing over sandbags in the model "Over the Top".

Arcadian Tommy with his machine gun, c.1914–30, l. 7cm/2¾in,
£55–65/$90–105

▼ Tommy with machine gun

When peace was declared production of many WWI models ceased, but this was one of the few that continued to be made for several more years. The rarest crested gun is the two-piece Savoy "Queens" or "Porcelle" on a tripod. Fairly scarce also are the Carlton British machine gun, with open and closed variations, and the Savoy British trench mortar gun. Many factories also issued menacing-looking howitzers.

Regional & national

Local customs, treasures and emblems were particularly significant to crested china manufacturers, and holidaymakers seized on these to take home as souvenirs of their visits. Welsh souvenirs included Welsh hats, leeks (inscribed with a Shakespeare verse), harps and spinning wheels. Scottish models ranged from bagpipes, and anvils from Gretna Green, to figures called "Souter Johnny" and "Tam O'Shanter" and Scotsmen in kilts. From Ireland came the elaborate "Irish Jaunting Car" with horse and driver, busts of an Irishman and Irishwoman, Irish harps, shamrocks and a "colleen" (girl) beautifully modelled by Carlton. Yorkshire and Lancashire are well represented, as the northern industrial townspeople took their "wakes weeks" (see p.28) in the northern resorts.

▼ **Cartoons**

Several firms issued pieces showing regional cartoons, with funny verses or stories printed on the reverse side. The cartoons included the "Yorkshireman's Advice" written in Yorkshire dialect, the "Hampshire Hog", "Somerset Cuckoo", "Trusty Servant", "Devonshire Dumpling", seen below, and "The Moonrakers". This last cartoon is the story of Wiltshire smugglers carrying illicit brandy who, when stopped by the Excise men, dumped their load in a pond and began raking at it with sticks. They claimed to be raking up the cheese from the moon's reflection.

Arcadian Devonshire dumpling, c.1903–33, ht 4.5cm/1¾in, **£20–25/ $30–40**

▶ **Welsh hats**

About 20 per cent of all crested Welsh hats are decorated with the letters of the longest place name in Wales. The name is printed around the brim, with the first letter usually illuminated. For those who wish to visit this famous Welsh town, the name is listed in most road maps of Britain as Llanfairpwllgwyngyll, in order to save space. Its full name, however, is Llanfairpwll-gwyngyllgogerychwyrndrobwll-llantysiliogogogoch. Many Welsh crests incorporate the red dragon of Wales and the Prince of Wales' feathers.

Savoy Welsh hat, c.1910–33, ht 5.5cm/2¼in, **£12–14/ $20–22**

Arcadian bust of Robert Burns, c.1903–33, ht 8.5cm/3¼in, **£60–65/$95–105**

▲ Robbie Burns

The writer and poet Robert (Robbie) Burns was a particularly popular choice for crested china, being issued as a Goss bust and coat-of-arms, and in any number of crested figurines. There is a figure group with "Highland Mary" as well as a "Burns Statue", "Burns with the Plough", busts, transfers and even models of his cottage in Ayr and his mausoleum. In the 18thC Burns was the best-known Scots bard; his poetry spoke of love, passion and friendship while his universal fame gave the Scots a national identity. The Burns legacy is immortal, and these Victorian and Edwardian souvenirs are still popular with collectors today.

▼ Crested china from Lincoln

Lincoln pieces are very collectable, and within that area are the following models: the "Cathedral West Front", "Stonebow", "Jacks" (the famous Lincoln imp) and tanks with the arms of Lincoln, which is where tanks were built. However, the "Devil Looking Over Lincoln", such as the Willow version below, is a misnomer with its City of Lincoln crest. Its origins were in fact Lincoln College at Oxford University, where a famous devil gargoyle overlooked the college. The statue was taken down in 1731, having previously lost its head in a storm.

Willow Art "Devil Looking Over Lincoln", c.1905–30, ht 11cm/4¼in, **£30–35/$50–55**

"DEVIL LOOKING OVER LINCOLN"

Carlton Irish colleen with spinning wheel, c.1902–30, ht 9.5cm/3¾in, **£45–55/$70–90**

▲ The Irish models

Ireland is very well represented by most of the potteries. Goss produced green shamrock transfers, and Carlton's "A Sprig of Shamrock" designs, shamrock-shaped dishes and harps were all popular. The rarest piece is the Irishman with a tiny pig standing by a milestone, on a base that reads "Don't be radin the milestones all day Alana".

Historical & folklore

Museums throughout Britain contain Roman, Saxon and Norman relics. These were copied first by Goss and then by many of the other manufacturers. Great care was taken to emulate the original, and often the crested copies name the original relic on the base. Most of the Goss models are now worth £5–10/$8–16. Collectors aim to acquire one of each, although few succeed as some are very rare, including the Cirencester Roman urn (£200/$320). Most of these artefacts are good value, and in today's market they represent a good investment. Events and heroes from history are immortalised, such as Joan of Arc, Lady Godiva on horseback, the bust of Peeping Tom, Mother Shipton, and the "Trusty Servant" from Winchester. Unusual souvenirs also include "Henry V's Cradle" from Monmouth, the "Leominster Ducking Stool", hinged with two pieces, and the "Westminster Coronation Chair".

▶ **Goss models**
Most of the 600-plus Goss models or artefacts were made between 1888 and 1934. Some of the models were made in a larger size during the earlier "first" period of the firm, and were later produced on a smaller scale. The large earlier pieces tend to be heavier, with thicker porcelain, weak gilding and paler crests, while the hue of the porcelain is more ivory than white. The Goss models made the firm famous, production of these artefacts dominating much of the factory's output. They were phased out in the early 1930s.

W.H. Goss Norwich urn, c.1885–1929, ht 6cm/2¼in, **£20–25/ $30–40**

▼ **The "Billiken"**
The "Billiken" was an American invention designed by Florence Pretz in 1908. A symbol of good luck, the cheerful little fellow with a bullet-shaped head was soon winging his way across the Atlantic to be picked up by designers in crested china factories. Each firm had its own ideas about how he should look, and so many versions were produced that they are reasonably priced in today's market. Here the "Billiken" sits on a throne above the crest for Herne Bay. The Goss factory never made "Billikens" as they were considered too frivolous.

Willow Art "Billiken", c.1905–30, ht 10cm/4in, **£12–15/$20–24**

▼ Thumbs up

This "Billiken" was modelled with his "thumbs up", either sitting on a throne, as below, or standing, with a wide moon-faced grin. In 1910 the "Billiken" became the mascot of St Louis University, USA after the school's football coach, Charlie "Moonface" Bender, who looked just like the popular little figure that had taken the USA by storm. The "Billiken" appeared as salt and pepper pots, belt buckles and pickle forks. In 1912 a female version, called a "Milliken", was introduced. Soon after that the craze for "Billikens" died down.

Carlton "Billiken",
c.1908–30, ht 8.5cm/3⅜in,
£12–14/$20–22

Willow Art "Man in the Moon",
c.1905–30, ht 5.5cm/2⅛in,
£22–28/$35–45

▲ Figures from folklore

Willow Art modelled the "Man in the Moon", which is sometimes found with a yellow-lustre face, and the "Man in the Sun", which is rarer, possibly because it is a complicated model with its pointed rays and was no doubt quite expensive. Other Willow folklore figures include the "Trusty Servant", the "Ripon Hornblower" and the "English Folksong Bride" standing by a chest – legend has it that she hid inside it, and was trapped there and died. The "Trusty Servant" was an image painted on a wall at Winchester College, the English public school; the accompanying verse describes him as the ideal servant.

▼ Boulogne sedan chair

The Carlton 17thC sedan chair is a more intricate design than the Goss example, and certainly rarer, but it is the Goss version for which collectors will pay more. There is just one known Goss model, painted turquoise blue, and this is probably worth over £300/$480. Sedan chairs have vulnerable handles, which are hard to repair if broken, and once damaged they are worth very little.

Carlton 17thC sedan chair,
c.1902–30, ht 7cm/2¾in,
£27–30/$43–50

Historical & folklore ~ 45

Sports & pastimes

Arcadian produced the best and widest sports and pastimes range. Three of the greatest sports at the end of the 19thC were cricket, golf and horse-racing. The golf-club head and the golf ball were made by several potteries, and Shelley produced a golf bag with clubs. Racehorses, with and without jockeys in coloured silks, were localised by crested arms. Cricket caps and bats are fairly rare, and the ultimate find for the cricket collector is the "Hambledon Cricket Stone" by Goss in grey parian (£1,000/ $1,600). Football offers trophies and balls, mostly by Willow Art – footballer ashtrays and figures are more rare. There are rugby balls, boxers and boxing gloves, and even billiard tables complete with balls and a cue. Pastimes include card symbols and indicators, folding box cameras and chess pieces.

▼ **Sporting ashtrays**

The combination of sport and the encouragement to smoke seems somewhat incongruous now. This footballer, dressed in a Chelsea strip, is kicking a ball outpressed with "Matches", which acts as a match-striker. Another ashtray on an octagonal base depicts the bookmaker, complete with greyhound and hare. Horse-racing is represented by a race-horse and jockey on a horseshoe ashtray inscribed "Humorist Winner of the Derby 1921 Donaghue Cup". Crown China produced a tennis player wielding a racket in front of a net, inscribed "40 Love", again on an ashtray base – painted green to represent the grass.

Arcadian footballer ashtray, c.1903–33, ht 11cm/4¼in, **£125–150/ $200–240**

▶ **Golf**

China golf memorabilia must have sold quite well because there are a number of golf balls around today, including salt and pepper shakers. This tiny caddie balanced on an outsized ball is a comical model. Another Arcadian model shows a diminutive caddie staggering under the weight of a giant bag of clubs. There is also a very rare figure of a golfer in his plus fours, standing ready to putt on an ashtray base, his outsized ball providing the match holder. At least one example of this piece has been found, oddly coloured in green and brown, with no crest.

Arcadian caddie, clubs & golf ball, c.1903–33, ht 7.5cm/3in, **£30–35/ $50–55**

▼ Cricket

Arcadian and Florentine made many cricket bags, in two different sizes, but not many bats, cricket caps or figures, and certainly no balls or stumps. One of the rarest cricket models is the Carlton cricketer holding his bat in front of the stumps awaiting the ball, on a base marked "Play M.C.C. The home of cricket formed 1787". This piece is probably worth £250–300/$400–480 to a cricketing fan. The cricket cap is made by only a few firms, such as Grosvenor and Rita China, while the best bats, being very small and delicate, are by Arcadian and Waterfall.

Arcadian cricket bag, c.1903–33, l. 8cm/3¼in, **£15–18/$25–28**

Botolph China billiards table, c.1914–25, l. 10cm/4in, **£175–185/$280–295**

▲ Unusual sports

Botolph and Arcadian produced identical billiards tables, both now very scarce. Other unusual sporting crested pieces are roller skates, curling stones, tennis rackets and the highly original figure, by Podmore, of a sprinter – a gangly athlete with a comical expression, kneeling on one knee on a narrow base. Of the different Boy Scouts made, Arcadian's and Willow's models are short and comical, inscribed "Be Prepared". The Tuscan Boy Scout salutes, and the finest Grafton versions are shown blowing a bugle and saluting.

Arcadian bishop chess piece, c.1924–25, ht 7cm/2¾in, **£18–25/$28–40**

▲ Hobbies

There are three sizes of chess piece – the most prolific medium set was by Arcadian-related potteries, the small are Wilton's, and the much larger pieces are by Corona. Very rare is the Grafton dice trump indicator, as on one side there is no trump. Folding box cameras by Arcadian and from Germany are highly sought after. Models were also made of stick telephones, the first type of phone.

Musical instruments

Few factories made musical instruments, so none are common, but of those made the more usual ones are the banjo, guitar, tambourine and harp. The Gemma tambourine with gilded cymbals is simply made, and Arcadian's version is very fine. Also highly sought after are the lute, double bass and violin, and there are several makes of drum, including a drum and symbol set by Saxony. Shelley's upright piano and Carlton's piano with open keyboard are both superb. Bagpipes are quite rare and can be found tied with white or bright turquoise china ribbons. Equipment such as the gramophone is included in this theme – Arcadian and Carlton both issued a fine gramophone in a cabinet, with a black record on the turntable, inscribed "Music hath charms", and Crown China made a smaller version.

▶ **Banjos**

The entertainer George Formby contributed to the banjo's popularity. Corona and Victoria China models were particularly large and heavily glazed, with bold lines of gilding depicting the strings on the banjo, the double bass and the harp. The Arcadian banjo comes in two sizes and is nicely detailed. The Willow model is much longer, as are its lute and guitar. Savoy's banjo is the rarest. Florentine's pierrot, with black pompoms on his hat, sits playing a banjo.

Arcadian tambourine, c.1903–33, diam. 5cm/2in, **£14–18/$22–28**

◀ **Tambourines**

The most realistic tambourine is the Arcadian piece illustrated left. The model showing the crest for Iceni has deeper sides and is more ivory coloured than this one. The Griffin China version is identical to Florentine's and Ivora's; most of Griffin's were made in the 1920s and are quite uncommon now, unlike Gemma's version. Of all of the musical instruments made there are more tambourines than any other. They were less expensive when originally sold because they were easier to manufacture. Many families played music, and most homes had a real tambourine.

Victoria China banjo, c.1910–24, l. 14cm/5½in, **£18–22/$28–35**

"Music Hath Charms"

Crested china record players are scarce. There are two versions of the record player in a cabinet, seen below, and both have black records. Box gramophones are more easily found. Some of the horn gramophones were marked "His Master's Voice" with an outline of a dog. This was "Nipper" (so named because he nipped the back of visitors' legs). In 1899 the gramophone company paid £50/$80 for a painting of Nipper listening to a gramophone, painted by his master Francis Barraud, and a further £50/$80 for the full copyright. "His Master's Voice" remains a well-known trademark today.

Carlton upright gramophone in cabinet, c.1902–30, ht 9cm/ 3½in, **£90–100/$145–160**

▼ Bells

Not much is known about the curious-looking bell illustrated below, but it must originate in Canterbury as it always shows that crest. Other china bells can be found with clappers, and they make quite a din when rung. Clifton made a suffragette hand bell marked "Votes for women, this one shall have a vote". Goss made two sizes of a Swiss cow bell with clapper. The Chertsey bell has a wooden clapper and wooden base, and is marked "Curfew must not ring tonight".

Arcadian "Campan Athome" bell, c.1903–33, ht 5.5cm/2⅛in, **£30–40/ $50–65**

▼ Historical instruments

This "Ulphus Horn" is a very rare piece (the original is in York Minster), and it comes on a base, as here, or on its own. Other related pieces are the "Ripon Hornblower", a figure blowing a horn, and one by Grafton that is often inscribed "The horn is blown every night at 9". The "Ripon Horn" by Carlton is a horn without a figure, sitting on a rectangular base, and this appears in two different sizes.

Carlton "Ulphus horn", c.1902–30, l. 11.5cm/4½in, **£25–30/$40–50**

Home nostalgic

Fascinating objects from the home, reproduced in china, provide a revealing insight into the way of life between 1890 and 1930. German potteries, which were quick to spot the British love of miniature everyday ware, flooded the market with kettles and teapots, minute tea sets, flatirons and shaving mugs. Almost all of the English factories also produced a range of nostalgic household ware. The fireplaces and ranges often have the mottoes "There's no place like home" and "East or West, Home is Best". Babies swimming, sitting or covered in paint with a paint pot were tricky to mould and expensive to buy. Hourglasses shaped as egg-timers, umbrellas, dustpans, saucepans and even a wedding ring are all highly collectable. There is a also a wide range of candlesticks, oil lamps and lanterns, as many homes still did not have electricity.

◀ **Clocks**

"Many of us are called but few get up" is the truism that appears on this piece. The rarest clock is the "Peace Clock" by Corona. With the hands at 3.25, it says on its central panel "Peace signed 3.25 June 25th 1919". This is now worth more than £75/ $120, as is a rare fob watch that lies flat. Grandfather clocks by British manufacturers are the most frequently seen, often with a colour transfer instead of a crest. Grafton's version of the grandfather clock is surprisingly rather plain, while other makers include interesting details.

Arcadian alarm clock, c.1903–33, ht 6cm/2¼in, **£18–25/ $28–40**

▼ **Verses**

Many crested shapes merit a verse like the one on this pillar box. Sundials come with "Life's but a walking shadow" and "Let others tell of storms and showers, I'll only count the sunny hours". A policeman with a raised hand to stop the traffic is printed with "A policeman's lot is not a happy one", taken from Gilbert and Sullivan's *Pirates of Penzance*. A thimble says "Tak A Thimble Full" and a lantern reads "Watchman What of the Night". "Whisky" and "Soda" bottles on a tray have the wording "The more we are together the merrier we will be".

Unmarked Florentine pillar box, c.1913–25, ht 7.5cm/3in, **£15–18/ $24–28**

• Coal-scuttles had many designs: Shelley's "Coal Hod" is labelled "Coal Rations, Yours to a Cinder!" (worth £10/$16).
• "Pillar Boxes" range from £10 to £25 ($16–40).
• A bust of an inebriated gent with a spotted bow tie and top hat is possibly of W.C. Fields and is now valued at £40/$65.

Carlton treadle sewing machine, c.1902–30, ht 8cm/3¼in, **£25–30/$40–50**

▲ "Modern" equipment

Crested china in the shape of "modern" equipment, like this Singer treadle sewing machine, is great fun. There is a cash register made by Saxony, but it is not as impressive as the Carlton version, which has printed keys and upright money signs. Saxony's typewriter is identical in mould to its cash register but labelled "My Little Typewriter". Radio operators, like the one illustrated on page 7, had variously sized microphones and horns, rectangular and square tables, and some were partly coloured. Radio horns (free-standing) can be found inscribed "Hello ... (town name) calling".

▼ Homely items

Familiar objects around the home were favourites to buy as souvenirs, particularly with the working classes. As well as fireplaces like the one below there were balls of string, coal-scuttles, cradles, dustpans, flatirons, stools, frying-pans and spinning-wheels. Outside the home, popular subjects were wheelbarrows, dog-kennels, sundials, village pumps with and without troughs, umbrellas, watering cans and even garden rollers.

Carlton fireplace with kettle, c.1902–30, ht 8cm/3¼in, **£25–30/$40–50**

Arcadian soda siphon, c.1903–33, ht 9.5cm/3¾in, **£16–18/$26–28**

▲ Alcohol

This was a big-selling theme and some expensive and unusual items like "The Nap Hand" (a hand holding coloured beer labels on a heart-shaped dish) were produced. There were many cheaper pieces as well, such as beer, champagne (pepper pot) and whisky bottles, beer barrels, beakers, wine glasses, ale pots, and soda siphons like the one illustrated above.

Shoes

From the 17thC men's and women's shoes have been styled to look different from one another, and during the "roaring twenties" of the 20thC, shoes became a serious fashion object. Best value among the crested china models are the saleable German imports with their variety in size, outrageous designs and bright colours. British potteries made shoes dating back to medieval times, with dainty pointed toes and frills to the top. Grafton's "oriental" shoes, Arcadian's "slipper wall pockets" with holes for hanging them on walls, Carlton's and Shelley's riding boots and Arcadian's "high boot" all added to the range. Goss had an excellent quality set of shoes, including "Norwegian", "Dutch sabot" and "Queen Elizabeth's riding shoe at Thaxted"; "Chile Spur" and "Chile Stirrup" are valued at £200/$320 and £100/$160 respectively.

"Mother Shipton" Lancashire clog, c.1902–30, l. 9cm/3½in, **£8–12/$13–20**

▶ **Mother Shipton**
The transfer on this Lancashire clog is in fact from Yorkshire. Legend has it that Mother Shipton was born in 1488 in a cave at Knaresborough as a summer storm raged. The nearby "petrifying well" (which has also been made in china) had the power to turn objects to stone, and Mother Shipton was blessed with special powers to see into the future. She predicted carriages without horses, men flying through the air, that "iron in the water shall float as easy as a wooden boat" and that "accidents will fill the world with woe".

▼ **High boots**
Not many firms attempted the high boot. Shelley made a detailed one, as did Carlton (illustrated below left), and Arcadian produced three different sizes. Boots made by Aynsley were usually emblazoned with military badges and are worth £50–70/$80–110. Pictured below right, the Grafton boot with puttee (cloth ties worn from ankle to knee by soldiers during World War I) balances beautifully on a narrow base. This piece is seriously underrated by collectors.

Left to right: Carlton riding boot, c.1902–30, ht 6.5cm/2½in, **£15–20/$25–30**; Grafton WWI boot with puttee, c.1914–20, ht 7.5cm/3in, **£22–25/$35–40**

• The rarest Goss shoe is the "Queen Elizabeth's riding shoe", worth £100–115/$160–185 with any crest, and £120–140/$190–225 with the Thaxted crest.
• Foreign shoes can be found in many colours, and some can be bought for just £5–10/$8–16.
• Shoes with open eyelets were laced and tied with brightly coloured ribbon, and some of these have survived today.

▼ The Queen Victoria slipper

The Queen Victoria slipper was originally sold with a paper leaflet outlining its story. Victoria's father, the Duke of Kent, went to live in Sidmouth in 1819 to benefit from the sea air and mild climate. A local shoemaker was commissioned to make his baby daughter's first shoes, but instead of making only two he made three and kept one as a momento. This third slipper is now in Sidmouth Museum, although the leaflet stated that it was then in the possession of the shoemaker's daughter – the wife of Goss' porcelain agent at Sidmouth.

W.H. Goss Queen Victoria slipper, c.1870–1929, l. 10cm/4in, **£25–30/$40–50**

German lady's heeled shoe, c.1920–39, l. 11.5cm/4½in, **£12–15/$20–25**

▲ 1920s shoes

Shoes were important to any "modern" young lady of the 1920s. Hemlines were shorter, unlike the modest full-length skirts of the Edwardian era, and shoes were more visible. "Flappers" liked to dance and party, so shoes such as the lustre heeled one above were typical of the time and embodied the modern spirit of the Jazz Age.

▼ Styles

In crested china there are shoes dating back centuries, like the "cracowes" of medieval times, with their impossibly long tapering points, the 1920s flapper's shoe and national shoes like the Dutch sabot. German-made souvenir-ware shoes like the one below are larger and brightly coloured. Some are lustred, others have heavily gilded bows and tassles, and others impossible heels. At the other end of the scale are plain white hobnailed boots and walking shoes, although these sometimes do have a ribbon or a bow picked out in blue.

German souvenir-ware yellow lustre slipper, c.1900–39, l. 13cm/5¼in, **£14–16/$22–26**

Hats

From the earliest times, society, class, status and gender dictated who should wear a hat and in what style. Hats were very much an everyday part of life in the era of crested china, but those that were most frequently modelled were the World War I, regional, religious, national, sporting, occupational, novelty and transport themes. Goss did not waver from its sober style to make caps and bonnets, but a scarce "Chile hat", curious in its flat appearance, is a sought-after Goss piece at £200/$320. Gemma's stylish contributions were a despatch rider's cap with silvered goggles, a bowler hat and a fireman's helmet. Boy Scout hats are rarely found named, and the Carlton "Saint Patrick's Mitre" is especially rare (£30–35/$50–55). World War I provides the richest range: the "officers' caps", "forage caps", scarce Savoy "RFC cap", "Territorial's hat" and overseas military hats.

Grafton Colonial soldier's hat, c.1914–33, l. 9cm/3½in, **£25–30/ $40–50**

▲ **Overseas military hats**
It has been said that when the Australian and New Zealand troops arrived at Gallipoli they wore their bush hats in the same wide-brimmed peaked-crown style. To avoid confusion the Australians rolled the brims. Savoy made an "Anzacs cap" with rolled brim and a "New Zealand hat". Carlton and Arcadian also both produced an "Australian hat" and a "Colonial hat" inscribed "Anzacs for ever".

▼ **"Useful" hats**
These hats by Gemma were termed "useful" hats, with their dual use of holding matches and having striking bases. There are only a few giant top hats – one of these is covered in flower transfers, and another has a brown umbrella on top. There is a giant unmarked nautical cap painted black, with the coat of arms painted inside. The giant-sized pieces were often used as shop display models.

Gemma top hat matchstriker, c.1900–39, ht 4.5cm/ 1¾in **£5–7/ $8–11**

Gemma despatch rider's cap with silvered goggles, c.1914–25, diam. 6.5cm/2½in, **£25–30/$40–50**

▲ World War I caps

Pictured above is Gemma's despatch rider's cap. Willow Art made a range of military hats, including the rare airman's cap, forage cap, glengarry, officer's peaked cap (one known is inscribed "Souvenir of Canadian Forces 1915"), *pickelhaube* or German military spiked helmet, as seen right, and "Tommy's steel helmet". Savoy produced a glengarry, a German steel helmet, a Romanian soldier's steel helmet and the unusual French trench helmet, as worn by the dauntless French *poilus* (soldiers).

▼ The glengarry

At the beginning of World War I those wearing soft headgear such as the glengarry and the forage cap suffered severe head injuries in battle. Steel helmets were subsequently given to the troops in 1916, and when they were in short supply the troops vacating the front line gave their hats to those taking their place. No doubt the Scottish soldier's kilt (as modelled by Carlton) was soon replaced also as being highly impractical for battle.

Arcadian glengarry, c.1903–33, l. 9cm/3½in, **£18–25/$28–40**

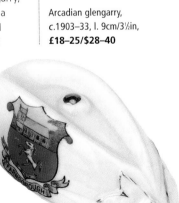

Willow Art *pickelhaube*, c.1914–30, ht 5cm/2in, **£30–35/$50–55**

▲ The *pickelhaube*

The *pickelhaube* is the name given to the German helmet worn at the beginning of WWI. However, it is far more likely that the Willow design, shown above, is based on a pre-war British military spiked helmet. The German design is certainly similar and was the standard item of military headgear for all German states, although it is most closely associated with Prussia.

Overseas

It was not until 1902 that Goss secured its first foreign agency, in Bermuda. By 1921 there were 186 overseas agencies in 24 countries (with 1,378 agencies functioning in Britain at this time). The large potteries such as Arcadian and Willow Art sold their products worldwide, and foreign arms appear on all sorts of shapes. Shelley had many Australian agencies, and produced a wide range of Australian transfers. Arcadian successfully exported small vases with the crests of French resorts, all factory-marked "Porcelaine Arcadienne". Foreign shapes were sold with any crest on, such as the Lucerne lion with the Blackpool arms. Goss flirted with models from other countries, with such diverse models as the "Russian Shrapnel Shell", "German Smoking Pipe", "Flemish Melk Pot" and "Antwerp Oolen Pot".

▼ **Norwegian models**
Popular Norwegian models include the dragon beer bowl, as seen below, the horse beer bowl and bucket, and the Norwegian shoe. The crest of any Norwegian town, such as Bergen or Trondheim, would be considered appropriate for these shapes, and the value would be two or three times more than if the crest were British. The two bowls and the shoe may come with the inscription in Norwegian, making them even more valuable.

W.H. Goss Norwegian dragon beer bowl, c.1890–1929, l. 15.5cm/6¼in, **£45–50/ $70–80**

▶ **New Zealand**
New Zealand agents chose some expensive shapes for their visitors to buy as souvenirs. New Zealand crests tend to appear not on the inexpensive little vases but on trams, kiwis (see right) and many unusual shapes such as this gold wedding-ring in a box. The comical statement on the box reads "Saftey First!". Where colour transfers were used instead of coats of arms they were outlined with black scroll borders. The major retail outlets in New Zealand were Frank Duncan Ltd in Auckland and Wellington.

Willow Art gold wedding-ring in box, c.1905–30, ht 6cm/2¼in **£30–35/ $50–55**

• Arcadian made a seated Japanese girl, valued at £50/$80. Shelley's standing "Japanese Lady", inscribed "Yum Yum", is worth £150/$240.

• Grafton's prized "doughboy" (American soldier), squatting and smoking a cigar, is valued at £200/$320.

• Small vases with foreign crests are inexpensive and could well increase in value. They can be found for £5/$8 upwards.

▼ Overseas models

British potteries tackled various overseas subjects, including the New Zealand kiwi bird pictured below. The majority of models made were war ones such as the Arcadian Belgian soldier bust and Russian cossack on horseback, and the Grafton American soldier, or "doughboy" as he was known, which was moulded crouching with arms around the knees, head on one side with hat at an angle, and a large cigar in the corner of the mouth. A rare German kiwi model exists, fully coloured in yellow and green, outpressed "Kiwi N.Z. no. 6527". Although coloured, it is worth only £40/$65.

Tourist Art China kiwi on base, c.1905–30, ht 6.5cm/2½in, **£70–75/$110–120**

Savoy jug, c.1914–18, ht 6.5cm/2½in, **£14–18/$22–28**

▲ Savoy WWI "pots"

Birks Rawlins & Co., the manufacturer of Savoy china, realised that the troops returning home from war wanted souvenirs to bring with them. The Savoy battle pots were the perfect choice. The crest is on one side, and the battle details are on the reverse. It was mainly the small vases that were decorated in this way, and only occasionally was a more intricate war model, such as a gun, decorated. Of course by the time the soldiers reached home, some of these war souvenirs looked as though they had been through their own battle.

▼ Unusual orders

This "Mannekin Pis" figure (modelled on the famous fountain in Brussels) was a daring piece to supply to the Belgian market. Its scarcity suggests that it was not the most popular choice of ornament to display on the mantelpiece. Willow Art also exported china to the Valentine & Sons agency in Cape Town under the trademark Disa Art China. The agency ordered small pieces – some animals, military items and miniature teapots. One unusual crest used was "The Municipality of the City of East London".

Florentine Brussels boy, c.1913–25, ht 12cm/4¾in, **£90–100/ $145–160**

Factory marks

Identifying crested china is easy when the pieces are factory marked. The major firms' marks are listed below. Many of these firms sold heraldic china for several decades, and the marks changed from time to time, so the most used example of each is drawn here. Other marks that can be found on the base need explaining: the gilded brush marks underneath the maker's mark were the gilder's own mark, so that any sub-standard gilding could be traced back to the culprit – the Goss pottery gave only three warnings before a gilder was dismissed; the coloured symbol was the mark of the paintress, who often spent several days colouring in part of a crest at a time, allowing a day for each enamel to dry, and marking her handiwork underneath in the last colour she had on her brush (the same procedure applied for any imperfect painting). These marks were fairly standard practice in the potteries, and most crested china shapes had their own symbols underneath. Retailers' marks were used when orders had been placed in advance. These have not so far added value to the pieces.

Goss

W.H.GOSS

The Gosshawk, used 1862–1927, was one of 28 variations

Alexandra

One of seven; china produced by several factories, eg Corona

Savoy

One of three marks; this one used mostly 1910–33

Shelley

One of seven used 1910–24; "Late Foley" added 1910–16

Carlton

One of eight; this was used on crested china 1902–30

Coronet Ware

This mark used c.1910–21; one other used up to 1924

Willow Art

One of twelve marks;
this one used 1907–25

Grafton

One of six versions; this mark
mainly used after 1915

Robinson & Leadbeater

One of four marks used;
this one 1900–1910

Austria

One of number of marks
used; no dates are known

Arcadian

There are eleven known
marks; this one used 1910–32

Foreign

One of 12; this used by German
and Austrian factories post-1918

Tuscan

One of two marks; this
one used 1906–25

Swan China

This is the only mark for
Swan China; used 1900–25

Saxony

Two marks, this one and the
word SAXONY. No dates known

Wilton

One of three marks; this
one used 1923–34

Gemma

One mark (no dates known);
"Fairy Ware" is alternative mark

Florentine China

This is the only known mark;
used 1900–25

Glossary

Artefact An object of archaeological interest

B.E.E. British Empire Exhibition

Bisque Hard paste biscuit porcelain

Coat of arms The heraldic shield of a person, a family or a place

Crest The modern term or slang name for a coat of arms; the crest is, more accurately, the heraldic symbol on the top of the coat of arms

Enamel A chemical colour that is painted onto the glazed porcelain and then fired in a kiln

Factory mark A pottery's individual printed mark, applied during manufacture to identify its wares

First period The earlier products of the Goss factory, from 1858 to 1887

Flapper 1920s name for a fashionable young woman

Gilding Edging with gold using a thin paintbrush

Glaze Hard thin glassy permanent film on the surface of the porcelain, rendering it impervious to liquid

Heraldic Armorial or crested

Impressed Marked with letters or numbers, stamped into the wet clay during manufacture

Miniature Representation on a very small scale, too small to use, for decorative purposes only

Monochrome One colour

Mould Shaped plaster-of-Paris cavity, made in two halves, into which liquid clay is poured to form the shape of the porcelain item; the mould is then removed

Nightlight Large hollow cottage made to hold a slow-burning light to act as a lamp

Parian A type of porcelain that can resemble marble; named after Paros, an island in the Aegean Sea, famed for its marble quarries

Plinth The base of a parian bust or statue

Polychrome Multicoloured

Porcelain Translucent vitreous ceramic material, usually white and thin

RFC/RNAS The Royal Flying Corps and the Royal Naval Air Service, which amalgamated in 1918 to become the Royal Air Force

Relief Numbering or marks in raised lettering

Reticulated Pierced

Second period The main era of the Goss factory, 1881–1934

Slip Creamy paste for coating and decorating pottery

Third period The later products of the Goss factory, from 1929 to 1939

Transfer Coloured permanent film, depicting a scene or view, applied to china

Traveller Factory representative who visited agencies to secure orders for crested china

Trim Gilding or coloured line around the rim of the china

Unglazed The parian shape without the waterproof glossy film of glaze